Copyright Claimed 2017

Acceptable Risk of Cancer
An Essay on Regulatory Policy

George E. Parris

I0414720

Abstract

This essay briefly summarizes the scientific errors in the linear, no-threshold (LNT) dose-response model for carcinogens, and explores the issue of the target for acceptable risk used to set regulatory standards by the US Environmental Protection Agency. While the LNT theory has been a regular topic of scientific criticism in scientific journals and elsewhere, the fallacies in the policy of setting targets for acceptable risk are less appreciated. The risk target used by the US Environmental Protection Agency (i.e., one-in-one-million *lifetime* risk of death) has its root in a brief, casual and fallacious conversation between to government bureaucrats. It is argued that the national target for acceptable risk is an issue that should be addressed by elected officials in Congress after through

Copyright Claimed 2017

debate rather than promulgated by rule by a government agency.

Divorced from science (contrary to Federal law), enforceable regulations from the EPA become the playground of conflicting political, emotional and economic interests. The combination of (i) the over estimation of risk from low-dose chemical exposure via the LNT and (ii) the excessively conservative targets for chemical risk management have created regulatory schemes that are economically destructive, suppress innovation and are (ironically) excessively risky.

Copyright Claimed 2017

Introduction

Many authors (Brues, 1958; Calabrese, 2013; Cuttler, 2009; Johnson *et al*, 2009; Lutz, 1998; Preston, 2003; Waddell, 2004) have criticized the use of the linear, no-threshold (LNT) dose-response model for cancer risk assessment. Indeed, the LNT model is based on a number of false assumptions and inappropriate extrapolations, which exaggerate calculated risk of exposure to chemical carcinogens especially at low-levels. When these *exaggerated estimates of risk* are compared to very conservative ideas of *acceptable risk* to promulgate enforceable regulatory standards, the resulting rules are economically destructive, suppress innovation and are (ironically) excessively risky. In this essay, I will call attention to the risk target used by the EPA and why it is so unreasonably conservative. I will also explain some of the factors that prevent the general public and informed public (e.g., the affected industries) from insisting on a more scientific basis of risk assessment and more reasonable risk targets.

Copyright Claimed 2017

A Brief Review of the Errors in the Linear, No-Threshold Risk Model

I have discussed the origin and errors incorporated in the LNT risk model for carcinogens in a full-length book. Here I only provide a brief summary and update: The LNT model has its origins in the work of Herman J. Muller (Muller, 1928a; Muller, 1928b), who conducted experiments with fruit flies in the 1920s. He noted that variations observable in the phenotype of the adult flies were associated with complex rearrangements of their DNA and that these "mutations" were produced as a linear function of the total dose (i.e., intensity x time)[1] of high energy x-rays.[2] He argued that in these experiments the complex DNA rearrangements inferred from changes in phenotype

---

[1] Intensity is the same as "dose rate."

[2] Photons are quantum phenomenon, not continuous. Each photon of the x-ray radiation (e.g., >1keV or 9.6×10^4 kJ/mole) studied by Muller carried enough energy to break hundreds of chemical bonds (e.g., 400 kJ/mole). The complex rearrangements observed under these conditions imply that the DNA sustained numerous *virtually simultaneous* double-strand breaks (DSB). The agent causing these breaks is presumably an intense shower of numerous reactive oxygen species (ROS) generated by radiolysis as the photon passes through the nucleus. **A single molecule of a chemical agent, does not have this ability**.

Copyright Claimed 2017

(caused by high energy x-rays penetrating directly into progenitor cells of larvae) seemed to have no threshold. Contrary to popular legend, Muller had almost nothing to say about cancer; he was primarily concerned with human population shifts by mutations resulting from radiation "fall out" from nuclear weapons and his claim was exclusively concerning *x-rays and mutations*. Indeed, he even mentioned contrary findings (radiation hormesis) by other experimenters using less energetic radiation (i.e., ultraviolet) in his Nobel Lecture in 1946:

> *"Moreover, as Altenburg (1930, 1935) showed, even the smaller quantum changes induced by ultraviolet exert this effect on the genes. They cause, however, only a relatively small amount of rearrangement of chromosome parts (Muller and Mackenzie, 1939) and, in fact, they also tend to inhibit such rearrangement, as Swanson (1944), followed by Kaufmann and Hollaender (1944 et seq.), has found."*
> H.J. Muller's Nobel Lecture (1946)

Without regard to the historical sequence of events, with the determination of the structure of DNA in 1953 by Watson and Crick (Watson & Crick, 1953a; Watson & Crick, 1953b), nuclear scientists in the 1950s made the leap (which was controversial at the time and still is) that damage to DNA cause either cell death or mutations *in future generations of*

Copyright Claimed 2017

the cell clone and that these mutated clones constitute the disease "cancer." Indeed, at the time (1950's), it was assumed that any molecule as complicated as DNA that was damaged must stay damaged (i.e., damage was irreparable). It was farther assumed that any mutated cell cone would not be subject to normal immune suppression by the host. Under these assumptions, an argument that there was a *linear, no-threshold* relationship between the *total dose of high-energy radiation (x-rays, gamma-rays) and cancer* could be rationalized.

However, these assumptions have been proven to be wrong (Pollycove & Feinendegen, 1999). First, we need to distinguish between massive rearrangements and simple single-base mutations. While massive rearrangements (e.g., chromothripsis (Stephens *et al*, 2011)) are not repairable and are known to contribute to cancer (Cai *et al*, 2014; de Pagter & Kloosterman, 2015; Forment *et al*, 2012; Meyerson & Pellman, 2011; Wyatt & Collins, 2013), simple single-base adducts (or similar damage) are readily repaired (Hoel *et al*, 1983; Swenberg *et al*, 1999; Yasui *et al*, 2014). The many mechanisms of DNA repair were not known until the 1960s and not fully appreciated until the 1980s. Similarly, the reproductive capacity of cell clones was assumed to be infinite until the 1960s and the importance of telomeres only

Copyright Claimed 2017

became fully appreciated around 2000 (Hayflick & Moorhead, 1961; Olovnikov, 1996). Finally, the mechanisms of apoptosis, which exert internal and external control on abnormal cells, was not understood until the 1980s and we are still learning about the ability of the immune system to induce apoptosis in abnormal cells (Prendergast, 2008).

Thus, simple point mutations are easy to repair and that is very important, because routine biophysical and biochemical process in cells (not involving exogenous factors) cause continuous damage to DNA, which is routinely repaired. *Although many chemical reagents are likely to form adducts with DNA bases or cause other direct damage to DNA and are judged to be "potential carcinogens," it seems very likely that chemical agents that interrupt the function of DNA repair or cellular apoptosis mechanism are more dangerous with respect to causing cancer than agents that introduce mutations* (Pollycove & Feinendegen, 1999). Since reactions that damage the molecules that are responsible for DNA repair or apoptosis follow typical biochemical mechanisms (having nothing to do with DNA), there is no reason to believe that they would be a linear, no-threshold function of dose of chemical agent.

Although we can excuse the original adoption of the LNT model by the EPA when it was founded (1970) because of

Copyright Claimed 2017

the contemporary ignorance of DNA repair, apoptosis and limitations of asexual reproduction on a cell clone because of telomere erosion, the extrapolation of the model used for high energy radiation to chemical exposure was as absurd then as it is now. Whereas radiation directly penetrates tissue and damages DNA buried in the nuclei of cells, chemical exposure (by dermal contact, ingestion, inhalation, or injection) must traverse a number of physical barriers and biochemical processes before reaching common target organs (bone, liver, bladder, kidney, pancreas, brain or even skin) (Yue *et al*, 2015). Indeed, it is clear that many carcinogens are subject to derivatization[3] (Klapacz *et al*, 2016) to enhance their excretion or require metabolic activation (Henkler *et al*, 2012) to react with DNA.

There never has been (since 1940) any reason to believe that these processes would follow a linear, no threshold dose-response curve. There has been some effort by the USEPA to incorporate physiologically-based pharmacodynamic modeling to estimate the actual dose of active carcinogen received by various tissues (Albert, 1994); but pharmacodynamics are not linear, and even if we could simulate the pharmacodynamics at relevant does-rates, it still does not resolve the DNA repair, apoptosis and

---

[3] For example, formation of adducts with cysteine (Liu *et al*, 2016).

Copyright Claimed 2017

telomere issues that are more critical to the existence of a threshold. And, of course, near toxic dose-rates in test animals cause fundamental dislocations of their metabolism (e.g., oxidative stress) favoring tumors independent of chemical reactions inducing genotoxity (Ames & Gold, 1990a; Ames & Gold, 1990b).

Most of these decontamination and activation processes are actually characterized by enzyme-facilitated Mechalis-Menten kinetics (Rupert, 1962). Under these conditions, experiments conducted at high dose rates (mg/kg/day) reach a saturated state, which *appear to be* independent of dose-rate and only depend on total dose (mg/kg). Thus, high-dose-rate (a.k.a., high-dose) animal exposure tests may obscure dose-rate-dependent effects at lower dose-rates that are typical of environmental or industrial exposure.

The preceding paragraphs merely summarize a variety of issues that make the *LNT model of cancer risk* biologically and chemically unsound. In practice, the only way to extract useful response behavior as a function of dose-rate at environmentally relevant concentrations in humans is from very careful epidemiological studies. The main limitation here is the difficulty in obtaining a large population and especially a large homogeneous population without confounding factors. Only the most potent carcinogens can

Copyright Claimed 2017

be evaluated this way. Probably the best controlled study ever done was done by the EPA focusing on exposure to arsenic in drinking water among Mormons (Cohen *et al*, 2013; Lewis *et al*, 1999). Ultimately, EPA rejected its own study on the basis that not enough people (several thousands) were studied and there were some minor inferences of confounding factors in the population. Thus, the attempts to reform the LNT risk model for regulatory decision-making have generally ended with a political agreement that the model is not good, but it is the "best available science," although I would not call it *science*.

Another twist on the use of epidemiology to identify risk from specific causes erupted in the literature in 2015 (Tomasetti & Vogelstein, 2015). In this case, the authors appear to follow the tack first taken by Ames (Ames & Gold, 1990a; Ames & Gold, 1990b) who deduced that incidence of tumors was enhanced by merely increasing the rate of cell division (mitogenesis) because of general toxic effects of chemical agents.[4] Tomasetti and Vogelstein argued that most (65% of) observed tumors were a result of

---

[4] In most animal cancer bioassays, the *maximum tolerated dose-rate* is used to obtain statistically relevant numbers of tumors. The toxic stress induces mitogenesis and leads to cancer. Then these cancer dose-response results are extrapolated to environmental exposure levels to project human risk at low dose-rates.

Copyright Claimed 2017

cumulative incidental DNA replication errors of stem cells acquired during cellular mitosis. For example, a plot of frequency of stem cell division rates in various tissues gave a linear correlation with incidence of cancer with an R^2 value of 0.65.

The argument of Tomasetti and Vogelstein is consistent with the work of Ames and Gold and both are clearly a threat to entrenched regulatory policies that focus on controlling environmental factors (e.g., chemical and radiological exposure). Thus, there were a number of immediate responses to the idea that "bad luck" was the principal cause of cancer. Some of these arguments attacked the applications of statistics (Tarone, 2015) and some attacked the entire idea of assigning causation to any one agent (Weinberg & Zaykin, 2015a):

> *"As we argued in our commentary, one cannot infer causality from an R^2 and cannot quantify the contribution of other factors by subtracting R^2 from 1."* (Weinberg & Zaykin, 2015b)

It is interesting that the same arguments are not applied when trying to tie observed cancers to specific manmade chemicals.

Copyright Claimed 2017

Recently the ability to efficiently sequence the DNA of tumors has revealed that many tumors contain evidence of chromothripsis (a sudden fragmentation of DNA (during one cell cycle) in a localized region of a chromosome). The original report estimated that only 2-3% of tumor genomes displayed chromothripsis (Stephens *et al*, 2011) and in hepatocellular carcinoma the frequency was found to be about 6% (Fernandez-Banet *et al*, 2014) but studies on bladder (Morrison *et al*, 2014), breast (Przybytkowski *et al*, 2014; Tang *et al*, 2015), colorectal (Kloosterman *et al*, 2011) and other cancers suggest that chromothripsis is a common early feature in the history of the malignant clones. Since chromothripsis is not caused by chemical genotoxicity or *low linear energy transfer* (low-LET)[5] radiation, they are presumably not common causes of complex mutations or cancer. I have suggested disintegration of potassium-40 (Moore & Sastry, 1982), which is concentrated in the nucleus and associated with DNA (Dick, 1978; Wilcox *et al*, 2008), as a likely source of chromothripsis. Muller noted that the terminal (high-LET, Bragg peak) impacts of photons and ions (i.e., *termini of electron tracks*) might account for the

---

[5] Low-LET radiation disperses energy and damage along its path instead of concentrating it in one spot, which is implicit in chromothripsis.

Copyright Claimed 2017

highly localized DNA damage he observed (i.e., complex mutations, chromothripsis).

The complex tasks of statistical analysis of epidemiological data and the assessment of cancer risk from controlled laboratory experiments have not proved fruitful in terms of modifying regulatory policy-making. Thus, this quandary brings us to the other issue that drives regulatory decision making and that is *acceptable risk*.

The History of Acceptable Risk in US Regulatory Policy

The Food and Drug Administration

Various standards for potentially toxic constituents contained in foods were introduced in British and American laws from around 1900. In the US, virtually all regulation by the Federal government is justified by the Commerce Clause of the Constitution, i.e., the option of the Federal government to establish laws that affect commerce among the states. In practice, having a national standard for environmental, health and safety regulations facilitates seamless production and sale of commodities through the

Copyright Claimed 2017

US and greatly influences international regulations because of the US's economic power since 1900.

The first relevant Federal health and safety regulation was the Pure Foods and Drug Act (1906), which focused on adulteration of foods by toxic substances. The regulations promulgated by the Department of Agriculture were driven by the idea that there was a threshold below which human intoxication was nil. By 1933 the law was being amended as the Federal Food and Drug Act and the word "risk" rarely appears and when it does appear, it is in the context of a binary accident; not a continuum of adverse effects.

This law continued (and continues) to evolve as new health issues arise. Typically, a specific incident that catches the public imagination is the motivations for expanding the scope and powers of Federal laws. For example, in 1932 a red organic dye called Prontosil was discovered to have anti-bacterial action. It was ultimately discovered that *in vivo* Prontosil was reduced to sulfanilamide, which was the active drug.

Prontisil had low solubility and was normally formulated as a pill; but its commercial success expanded in the general population after it was used successfully to cure the son of Franklin D. Roosevelt in 1936. This notoriety soon prompted the S.E. Massengill Company of Bristol,

Copyright Claimed 2017

Tennessee to create a raspberry-flavored/red-colored "elixir of prontosil" in diethylene glycol (the only feasible solvent) targeted at families for use in children. Although the drug was regarded as safe, this company did not stop to think that the unusual organic solvent necessary to dissolve it (i.e., diethylene glycol) might be toxic. There was no contemporary requirement for efficacy or safety testing. As over 100 deaths were reported to the Food and Drug Administration, it was soon determined what the problem was. The company thought they had followed the law as it existed at that time: The product was pure and its label was chemically accurate (10% drug, 72% diethylene glycol, 16% water).[6] Nonetheless, under the existing FDA law, the term "elixir" was reserved for materials dissolved in *ethanol*. FDA was able to take action against the *mis-branded drug* and the company based on this violation (1938). More importantly, the FDA legislation was promptly expanded as

---

[6] Independent of any safety statute, the company was successfully sued under tort law (gross negligence). Other companies had apparently had the same idea but were more cautious and abandoned their projects.

Copyright Claimed 2017

the 1938 Federal Food, Drug and Cosmetic Act to require safety testing (Wax, 1995).[7]

With regard to food additives (intentional or unintentional), it was assumed that poisonous materials followed a conventional S-shaped dose-response curve (i.e., an integration of a bell-shaped distribution of sensitivity of the exposed individuals) as shown in the figure below. The no observed effect level (NOEL) is a practical threshold for the population and the FDA typically set the maximum allowable concentration of food additives at 1/100th of this level after considering the amount of food that might be eaten in a day (i.e., Allowable Daily Intake, ADI).

---

[7] The law was later expanded in 1962 by the Kefauver-Harris Drug Amendments to require efficacy testing.

Copyright Claimed 2017

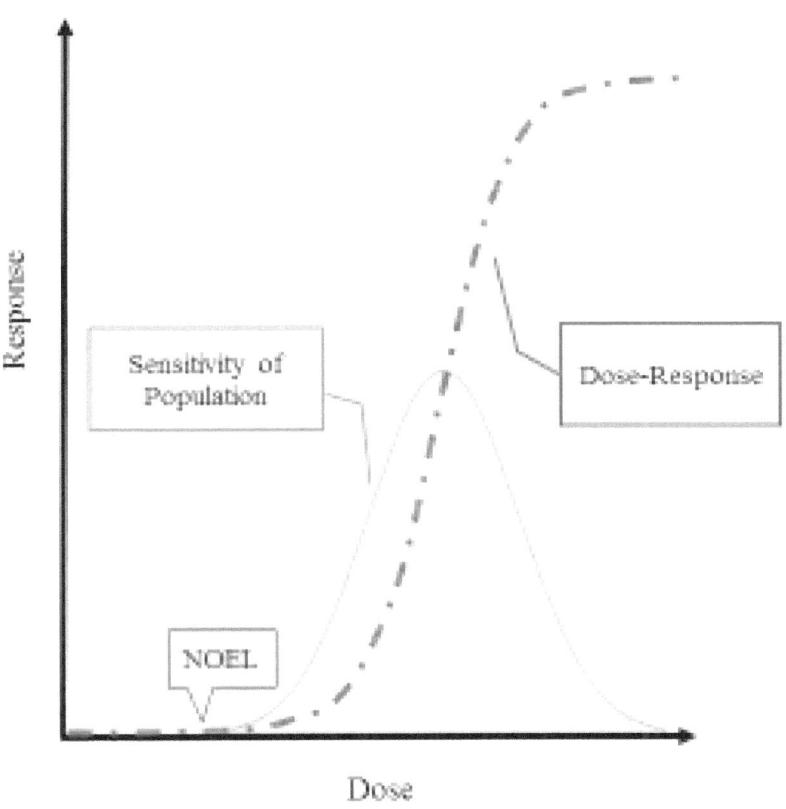

World War II had an unexpected impact on risk analysis. The concept of strategic bombing (i.e., targeted bombing of industrial facilities to disrupt military production) gave rise to the analysis and projection of bomb damage as an element in the field of operations research (Rau, 2005). This analysis technique crept into the analysis of radiation-induced mutations and Muller's "hit" terminology of radiation effects. In his 1946 Nobel lecture, Muller (Muller,

Copyright Claimed 2017

1928a) was summarizing data from a number of other scientists (Oliver, 1930) who had examined the relationship between mutations and radiation:

> *"They leave, we believe, no escape from the conclusion that there is no threshold dose, and that the individual mutations result from individual "hits", producing genetic effects in their immediate neighborhood. Whether these so-called "hits" are the individual ionizations, or may even be the activations that occur at lower energy levels, or whether, at the other end of the scale, they require the clustering of ionizations that occurs at the termini of electron tracks and of their side branches (as Lea and Fano point out might be the case), is as yet undecided."* H.J. Muller's Nobel Lecture (1946)

Repair of bomb-damage on industrial infrastructure had clearly been understood and observed during WWII. Indeed, it had driven the frequency of repetitive bombing of immovable industrial facilities (e.g., Ploesti oil refineries). Nonetheless, at the time of Muller's Nobel lecture (1946-1953), the structure of DNA was unknown, and the processes of DNA repair were unimaginable. Thus, it is easy to see how a linear, no-threshold model *for mutations* would seem reasonable. This hypothesis was tested and

Copyright Claimed 2017

appeared to be justified by experiment (Spencer & Stern, 1948).

While Muller himself was primarily concerned with the effects of mutations on the human population, the extrapolation from mutations to cancer was being pushed by others (1937; Berenblum & Shubik, 1949; Burdette, 1951; Burdette, 1953; Burdette, 1954; Burdette, 1955). And a *multi-hit mutation hypothesis* was proposed (Nordling, 1955) to account for cancer. This approach was quickly adopted in post-war years to estimate the impacts of radiation following the introduction of nuclear weapons.

The application of the LNT hypothesis of mutation and cancer was extrapolated from radiation to chemical exposure between 1946 and 1965 (Auerbach & Robson, 1946; Brookes & Lawley, 1964a; Brookes & Lawley, 1964b; Carr, 1949; Haddow, 1974; Hadorn & Niggli, 1946; Magee & Schoental, 1964; Orgel, 1965).

While all this was going on, the Food and Drug Administration received new and drastic guidance from an uninformed Congress in the Food Additives Amendment of 1958. Representative James J. Delaney (D, NY) managed to get a naïve clause inserted into the part of the legislation that instructs how food additives shall be evaluated:

...no additive shall be deemed to be safe if it is found to induce cancer when ingested by man or animal, or if it is found, after tests which are appropriate for the evaluation of the safety of food additives, to induce cancer in man or animal...

Superficially logical, the so-called "Delaney clause" disallowed any chemical found to be carcinogenic in humans or animals (or after *appropriate*[8] biochemical testing) from use as a food additive (or unintentional residue in food). The unexpected first impact of the Delaney clause was to ban a large amount to the cranberry sauce containing residues of the herbicide aminotriazole (recently determined to be carcinogenic) just before Thanksgiving in 1959. The Delaney clause's impact was soon to grow exponentially because of rapidly improving sensitivity of

---

[8] Although a logical application of the clause would challenge the appropriateness of tests, no bureaucrat or defendant is willing to take on this burden. We see exactly the same capitulation under the CERCLA legislation where regulatory requirements for environmental remediation are required to *applicable or relevant and appropriate* (ARARs). Although this standard has been provided by Congress, virtually any requirement is enforced without debate. You can guess that a law passed by Congress will be abused by the regulatory agency if it has the term "appropriate" in it. The implementing agency (EPA, FDA) will suppress challenges under this criterion because they are the recognized authority of "appropriateness."

Copyright Claimed 2017

chemical analytical techniques (1960-1980)[9] and the large number for chemicals being tested in animals for carcinogenesis under extreme conditions (i.e., maximum tolerated dose for life). These factors combined to make the Delaney clause a constant source of regulatory stress until it was finally modified in 1996 by passage of Title IV of the Food Quality Protection Act, which removed pesticide residues from its scope.

In the 1950s, it was realized that the LNT model allowed creation of a dose-response "curve" that would allow projection of risk at low doses (i.e., dose-rates) by extrapolation beyond the range of the original experiments. Thus, animal bioassays could be conducted at maximum tolerated dose-rates (e.g., mg/kg/day) and (after some allowance for differences in metabolism between, e.g., mice and humans and application of some sort of a safety factor) a projection of risk at very low levels could be made. Note that since the dose-rate was normally held as a constant in animal bioassays, the total dose (e.g., mg/kg) over a period of time is just a linear function of the dose-rate (total dose = dose-rate x time). Thus, the conceptual tool to identify

---

[9] In 1958, chemical analyses were typical in the 1/1000 level, but by 1980 there were routinely at the 1/1,000,000,000 level for pesticide residues. This made the term "no additive" very potent.

Copyright Claimed 2017

carcinogens fell into place in the 1960s. When the US EPA was established in 1970, the agency was soon under pressure to use it to set enforceable standards.

The Environmental Movement

Meanwhile a broader environmental movement was taking root in the US. Through the 1950s, chemistry and the chemical industry were viewed as a major benefactor of the US economy and the health and standard of living of the American public. Synthetic rubber, synthetic fibers (e.g., nylon, polyester), plastics (e.g., poly-olefins), antibiotics, high octane gasoline, and pesticides (e.g., DDT) all were clearly great positive steps forward and no down-side was anticipated before 1960. For example, with great optimism, a combination of DDT (to kill mosquitoes) and chloroquine (to kill the protozoa) were selected as a two-pronged attack on malaria by the World Health Organization in 1955. Soon, tons of the pesticides and drugs were applied in endemic malaria areas (D'Alessandro & Buttiens, 2001). But all was not well. In some places, the combination of DDT and chloroquine was effective in eradicating malaria, but in the Congo basin it was a failure.

Copyright Claimed 2017

In 1956 methylmercury poisoning (Minamata disease) was reported in Japan as a result of industrial pollution. The phenomenon of bioaccumulation was recognized as fat-soluble organomercury compounds moved from the water column into sea food and then into humans. The persistence of pesticides like DDT (once considered to be a major asset) began to come into question as a possible problem in the food chain. By 1960, it was apparent that wide-spread antibiotic resistance was occurring as penicillin and chloroquine became less effective. It was also apparent that pesticides were killing non-target species.

Into this arena stepped an unlikely champion, Rachael Carson. She was a successful and popular biologist/naturalist and science writer focusing on nature topics. Unbeknown to the public or her critics, she developed breast cancer in 1960 and was treated with radiation and chemotherapy until her life ended in April 1964 at age 56. The influence of her painful cancer on her focus on pesticides has been debated and is not clear; but it would not be unusual for a person with an incurable disease to look for causes. Clearly, by 1960 the connection between chemicals and cancer was in the scientific literature to which she had access. Regardless, she wrote a book about a subject that she was well-qualified to discuss, i.e., the

Copyright Claimed 2017

impact of persistent pesticides (especially DDT) accumulating in the food chain on top-level predators (insect-eating/fish-eating birds). She called her book *Silent Spring* alluding to a hypothetical absence of bird songs in the spring. The book was an instant popular success. While the science in the book was weak and not original to Carson (Dewitt *et al*, 1955; George & Mitchell, 1947), her logic was appealing and it certainly struck a chord with anyone with obsessive compulsive tendencies (e.g., inherent chemophobia). Thus, DDT became the target of a growing anti-chemical movement.

Nonetheless, the absence of a clear scientific basis for regulatory action of DDT resulted in a prolonged and hotly contested debate about the use of DDT, which was not banned until 1972. The scientific basis was ultimately provided by scientists who found a link between the thinning of raptor egg shells and reduction in population of large bird species (Bitman *et al*, 1969; Menzie, 1972; Moore & Walker, 1964; Peakall, 1969; Ratcliffe, 1967). These scientists founded an environmental lobbying group known as the Environmental Defense Fund (EDF) in 1967 to press their case (Odum *et al*, 1969; Woodwell *et al*, 1967).

The case against DDT was vastly aided in the 1960s by the commercial introduction (in 1962) of the electron capture

Copyright Claimed 2017

detector for gas chromatography. This detector provided high sensitivity and great selectivity for organohalogen compounds and made routine analysis of environmental and biological samples for traces (i.e., sub-part-per-million levels) of halogenated compounds fast and inexpensive. The search for DDT residues had an interesting and unexpected side effect: A wide variety of other halogenated pesticides (lindane, chloradane etc.) were detected in the same samples as DDT and ominously a group of compounds that were not pesticides were also detected. The non-pesticide industrial chemicals showing up in environmental samples were led by polychlorinated biphenyls (PCBs), a mixture of over 100 individual compounds and isomers produced by chlorination of biphenyl (Peakall, 1972; Risebrough *et al*, 1968). PCBs (like DDT) were at the time considered essentially non-toxic in humans and were widely used as fire-proof dielectric fluids in transformers in the electrical distribution grid and heat transfer fluids. They were handled haphazardly and disposed without concern. Unfortunately, PCBs also were persistent and bioaccumulated.

In 1967, the Santa Barber, CA oil spill prompted Congress to pass the National Environmental Policy Act (NEPA), which required Federal agencies to conduct environmental

Copyright Claimed 2017

assessments and, if warranted, prepare and file (for public scrutiny) full environmental impact statements (EIS) before undertaking major federal projects. The EIS was designed to ensure that the agency considered the environmental impacts of a series of reasonable alternatives and that these impacts were disclosed to the public. However, the agency is still allowed to make a decision that has adverse environmental impacts based on economics and other considerations. The USEPA was founded on this legislation (1970) with the idea that it would become the focus of efforts to protect human health and the environment from pollution. NEPA legislation opened the door for aggressive environmental lobbying and resulted in the founding of the Natural Resources Defense Council (NRDC) in 1970. The NRDC has routinely used litigation based on compliance with NEPA to force government agencies to produce EISs and then lobby to have the analyzed alternatives limited to those that the NRDC considers acceptable. If the agency pursues an alternative that was not analyzed during the EIS, the agency is in violation of NEPA and is subject to farther litigation. Thus, most NEPA litigation is on procedural issues not necessarily scientific issues.

The finding of numerous industrial chemicals (i.e., not registered pesticides) incidental to the study of DDT in

Copyright Claimed 2017

environmental and biological matrices ended the assumption that these compounds were automatically and naturally degraded in the environment. It set motion two paths of regulation: control of industrial chemicals and control of waste disposal. The first legislation that emerged from this analysis was the Toxic Substances Control Act (TSCA). By the time I arrived at the USEPA[10] (401 M St SW Washington, DC, late spring 1976), the Office of Toxic Substances consisted of about 40 people focused on getting the legislation passed by Congress. I worked for a branch dedicated to finding examples of environmental pollution by industrial chemicals. PCBs had already become the poster-child arguing for passage of the legislation: It was manufactured in large quantities; it was released through manufacture, use and disposal; it was persistent in the environment; it bioaccumulated; and there was relatively little testing data available to assess its toxicity.

---

[10] I had been an NRC post-doc at what is now NIST (Department of Commerce); but when my appointment was ending, I was hired by NIST and sent on detail to EPA-OTS essentially as a spy to find "testing" work for NIST. Unfortunately for NIST, the testing that EPA was planning was bioassays, which was not within the mandate of NIST. I became a full-time employee of EPA shortly after TSCA was passed.

Copyright Claimed 2017

TSCA became law October 11, 1976 and my management focused my efforts onto polybrominated biphenyls (PBBs), which had already been responsible for a major incident in Michigan where it was accidentally mixed into feed for dairy cows (1973). That episode had mainly involved the FDA and Department of Agriculture. It is relevant that Jimmy Carter (D) won the presidency over Gerald Ford (R) in November 1976 and as soon as he was inaugurated in January 1977 the leadership of EPA and especially OTS began to change.

Many Democrats in Congress had felt that the Republican leadership of EPA/OTS was reluctant to use the powerful tool that had been given to them in TSCA.[11]

---

[11] This motivation had an unanticipated effect on me. As the Carter Administration took charge in the spring of 1977, I was tasked to demonstrate human exposure to PBBs. Time constraints prevented obtaining permissions for collecting human samples in the normal way (blood, urine). I had the brain storm to collect human hair from barber shops near manufacturing facilities and this was done by a very competent contractor. Interestingly, we indeed found PBBs in various hair samples. This was big news and led to a news conference (June 17, 1977) where I reported the results (I did not realize I was a superstar of EPA's drive to expand the use of TSCA). The next task that was assigned to me was to show food chain contamination by PPBs. Unfortunately, the contract with the original contractor was ended and my branch chief moved the work to a different (must less competent) contractor. I secured the assistance of various state fish

Copyright Claimed 2017

---

and wildlife teams and had cat fish collected from the Ohio River near Cincinnati (which was downstream of a known PBB-user plant in Parkersburg, WVa). The fish were delivered to the new contractor about July 5th and I waited for the results, which arrived by air-express on Friday night July 29th 1977. There was some push from above but, I did not know what prompted the urgency. The contractor's report essentially said that they had found high levels (part-per-million levels) of PBBs in the fish, but provided little scientific support for the claim. I reported the findings to my branch chief by memo Monday August 1st but noted that the levels were so high that I had some reservations about them. Indeed, I included the following caveat in my memo to my branch chief:

> "I personally will not stand behind this data until it is confirmed by full scan GC-MS and I would like to have the retention times of the three (commercially available) isomers of monobromobiphenyl compared to the peaks observed in the samples. I recommend these data not be "advertised" until confirmation is completed. Full scans will hopefully be available by Tuesday (August 2, 1977)."

Although the lab was using GC-MS with multiple ion monitoring and signals appeared on each of the three masses selected to be sensitive to PBBs, they did not provide a full scan mass spectrum (which would be confirmatory and should have been easy to obtain considering the levels they were reporting). I was not aware why the time pressure was so great; but I soon found out. I was invited to attend (not testify) at a House Oversight Committee hearing (August 2-3) in which the acting Office Director (a biologist whom I had not briefed) gave a general overview of how the EPA/OTS was proceeding to implement TSCA. The committee was particularly concern that the EPA/OTS was not applying the imminent hazard and other regulatory provisions of TSCA to immediately stop production of chemicals of interest. Then the microphone was moved to Representative Tom

Copyright Claimed 2017

Luken (D) from Ohio 1st Congressional District (which included Cincinnati) and the lights for TV cameras came on (obviously pre-planned) the Congressman announced (to my great surprise and I suspect to the office director's) that the committee had been informed that the EPA/OTS had found high levels of PBBs in Ohio River Catfish and he was demanding to know what EPA/OTS planned to do about it. The office director (with my branch chief at his elbow, both sworn to testify under oath) proceeded to (incorrectly) characterize the findings as a problem in quantification...i.e., he implied the identity was known and all we had to do was pin-down the concentration. In fact, I was not convinced that PBBs had been found. By the time we returned to the office, I was being pressured to "confirm" the findings. The contractor was so incompetent that they continued to insist that they had the results, although they did not provide me with the one piece of information that I would consider conclusive (i.e., the full scan mass spectrum showing the characteristic peaks of PPBs). The results of the hearing made the *Washington Post* and I soon received a call from the FDA, which supported my skepticism. It turned out that FDA had a lab at 200 C St SW and following the original PBB episode in Michigan, they had monitored Ohio River and Mississippi River cat fish for a variety of pesticides and industrial chemicals. They were chemists and knew what they were doing. I also ran the available results past other contractors I had and all were willing to say that there was no evidence for PBBs in the chromatograms they reviewed. Finally, I received a full scan mass spectrum from the contractor and it was apparent that whatever the peak was, it was not PPBs. Farther investigation indicated that it was "fish fat" coming through *en masse* and that virtually every specific ion mass (including the three originally used by the contractor) showed a response! The contractor had not done an adequate clean-up of the original extract and had foolishly defended their initial conclusions. To make a long story short, I soon left the highly political

Copyright Claimed 2017

My car pool to EPA/OTS from the suburbs included Frank Kovar (future OTS division director) and Charlie Auer (future office director 2002 to 2009, retired in 2009 after 32 years with EPA). After passage of TSCA, speculation was wild that the scope of TSCA was so broad that it would be spun off as a separate agency and moved to Gaithersburg, MD were we all lived. Indeed, TSCA could have incorporated the task now covered with the Resources Conservation and Recovery Act (RCRA) and the Comprehensive Environmental Response, Compensation and Liability Act (CERCLA, a.k.a., Superfund). But, for a variety of reasons, Congress moved separate legislation for RCRA (became law October 21, 1976) to address disposal of waste materials.

The public motivation to deal with legacy waste sites[12] was not in place until the Love Canal episode (1976-78), This

---

atmosphere of the EPA for a science-based job at the FDA. Ironically, the incoming office director actually liked my work and I was encouraged to stay. Several months later EPA/OTS corrected the original testimony to Congress.

[12] Dealing with contamination that had already occurred is a tricky problem. Specifically, when the waste dumps (such as Love Canal) were created, it was legal. Indeed, in the case of Love Canal the original owners provided fairly sophisticated paperwork to free

Copyright Claimed 2017

facilitated the passage of CERCLA (December 11, 1980). Addressing legacy waste contamination issues was tricky because of the Constitutional prohibition of *post hoc* laws. The episodes that produced contaminated soil and water before 1980 were legal at the time they occurred. Thus, the law provided a special tax on certain industrial chemicals (i.e., superfund) to fund EPA's remediation of these problems. The initial remedial targets were, in fact, based on risk assessment using target acceptable risk discussed below. But risks can be managed by isolating contaminated media from people as well as eliminating the contaminated

---

themselves of civil liability even in the absence of a law. To circumvent this issue (US Constitution Section 9 (3): 3: *No Bill of Attainder or ex post facto Law shall be passed.* Also see Section 10(1)), Congress created a special tax on certain industrial chemicals that went into a pool called "the superfund" that was to be used by the USEPA to remediate legacy sites. The law (CERCLA) granted the EPA authority to access private property to investigate and remediate, but the actual cost was to be paid by the government. Presumably the 5th Amendment would also apply to EPA actions: ... *nor shall any person .... be deprived of life, liberty, or property, without due process of law; nor shall private property be taken for public use, without just compensation.* Nonetheless, the superfund soon proved completely inadequate and there was a period of time (1980-early 1990s) during which the EPA pursued a policy of "polluter pays," to which many corporations and individuals acquiesced. It was not until the Clinton Administration's overreaches that a line was drawn in the sand by potentially responsible parties (PRPs) and EPA began acknowledging the date of enactment of CERCLA in naming and suing responsible parties.

Copyright Claimed 2017

media. Since it is far less expensive to control exposure by prohibiting land/water uses than by remediating the contamination (to essentially non-detect levels), most of the early (1980-86) remedial plans favored control strategies.

Thus, when the Superfund Amendments and Reauthorization Act (SARA) were passed in 1986, the statute was modified to require that the remedial plan ensure that the remediated site comply will all *applicable or relevant and appropriate requirements* (ARARs), *regardless of risk to the demonstrably exposed population*. For example, the drinking water standards (maximum contaminant levels, MCLs) were applied as targets for remediation of virtually all contaminated groundwater. This became a particularly draconian standard and one which was greatly abused.

The abuse of ARARs was particularly pernicious because many of the caveats present in the proposed standards were not understood or were intentionally disregarded by those determining what the ARARs were. That is, some of the rules driving remedial design (in lieu of any risk) were not actually *applicable or relevant and appropriate*. For example, if you read the drinking water standards, you find that they only apply to municipal drinking water systems above a certain size. These systems must meet certain unrelated practical as well as statutory requirements. For example, no

Copyright Claimed 2017

one is going to establish a municipal drinking water system (i) using a shallow aquifer (just below the surface of the soil where bacterial contamination is likely) without a water treatment system or (ii) which cannot produce the rate of water needed (gallons per hour) or (iii) does not have the long-term capacity (total volume or recharge rate) needed for a municipal system. Even private domestic wells take these issues into consideration. Nonetheless, it became routine under CERCLA-SARA for *any amount* of contaminated water (e.g., small pockets of contaminated water perched above impermeable layers) to be required to meet the drinking water MCLs as though they were "relevant and appropriate requirements." It should have been argued that the drinking water MCLs were neither applicable, nor relevant nor appropriate standards for remediation of pockets of "perched water," but since few people ever looked into the MCL background, the strict standards were simply incorporated as remedial targets into the remedial plans.

The Resource Conservation and Recovery Act (RCRA) standards posed an even more pernicious burden associated with implementation of CERCLA. Under RCRA the EPA had attempted to outlaw mere dilution as a way to avoid disposal regulations. To do this they created a list of

Copyright Claimed 2017

industrial waste streams that were presumed to meet the criteria for "hazardous waste" contained in RCRA. The EPA then administratively circulated (without promulgation) rules that effectively required that is these *listed wastes* were mixed with, contained in or treated to produce a residue (i.e., something was derived from the listed waste) these materials would be considered to be hazardous waste regardless of concentration of individual contaminant. And, the materials would be subject to the same regulations regarding disposal and management as the original listed waste. The problem arose that under CERCLA, release of hazardous substances (including RCRA hazardous waste) to the environment made a person subject to CERCLA "strict joint and several" liability. Basically, in the process of investigating or remediating a contaminated site, a contractor could (in principle) be held liable for remediation of the entire site if they dug up a shovelful of contaminated soil and tossed it back on the ground. Chaos reigned any time lawyers got involved with environmental remediation projects (at least through 1996 when I left the business).

Copyright Claimed 2017

What are EPA's Risk Targets and Where did they come from?

While the principal debate regarding risk assessment policy has addressed the science and technology of risk assessment (as discussed above), very little attention has been given to determination of acceptable risk (i.e., the risk that trigger precautionary action). I believe that the underlying reason for the lack of debate is that the targets that were set by the USEPA are so unreasonably strict that the environmental lobby has had nothing to complain about and the business and academic interest have generally steered clear of a potential political controversy. In the 1970s, the FDA was dealing with the effects of the absolutist "Delaney clause" which was essentially a *zero-risk* action level so whatever came out of the USEPA (in the 1970s) would look moderate by comparison. According to Roy Albert (Albert, 1994), who was a high ranking EPA official, the default USEPA cancer risk assessment target for action was set during a casual meeting in a hallway between two bureaucrats with little or no thought to its impact or relevance. The target risk for USEPA cancer risk regulation is *10^{-6} deaths per lifetime of exposure* (see for example, target risk criteria in CERCLA: 40CFR300.430(e)(2)(i)(A)(2)):

Copyright Claimed 2017

The most commonly used target risk is an excess lifetime incidence of 10^{-6}. This risk level had its origins in the EPA in the late 1970s when the Chairman of the CAG[13] was asked by the then-head of the Water Office in EPA, in a hallway conversation, for a suggestion of what a target risk might be that could be used as a recommendation to the states as the basis for their developing standards for the contamination of water bodies with carcinogens. The response was that excess lifetime cancer risk might be appropriate because this is about the level that seems to be ignored by the general public in relation to the risks of getting killed in mass transportation accidents. The recommendation that was finally issued was a range of 10^{-5} to 10^{-7}. It was a small jump to split the difference and come to a value of 10^{-6} for the cleanup of hazardous wastes. (Albert, 1994)

It is not clear exactly where the 10^{-5} came from, but the frequency cited by Albert is actually the acceptable risk *per trip* (e.g., the probability that a trip in public transportation will involve a death); *not per lifetime.* The USEPA reduced

---

[13] Roy E. Albert MD was the chairman of CAG (the Cancer Assessment Group) that was given agency-wide authority over cancer risk issues. The CAG was formed as a recommendation of the *Interim Procedures and Guidelines for Health Risk and Economic Impact Assessments of Suspected carcinogens* (May 26, 1976).

that by an order of magnitude to 10^{-6} and made it the tolerable risk for a life-time of exposure to carcinogens.

Assuming that the 10^{-5} risk number is correct (I have not found corroboration), the subtle and ultimately absurd move from *per event* to *per life-time* was a very important change of perspective. If (indeed) the public finds a 10^{-5} risk of death in *a single airplane* flight to be acceptable, what is the actual life-time risk they accept? A very occasional traveler will likely make 5 round trips (10 flights) in a life-time and a business person might make a round trip ever week for 20 years or on the order of 2,000 individual flights in a life-time. Thus, the actual acceptable risk that Albert and his colleague should have considered would range from 10^{-4} to 10^{-2} *per lifetime*. Let me suggest focusing on a more common and universal mode of transportation: automobiles.

People routinely drive their cars (or ride as passengers in cars) for *hundreds of thousands of miles in their life-time.* Remarkable improvements in automobile safety (e.g., airbags, anti-lock brakes, stability controls, traction controls) have lowered fatalities in recent years to *1.15 deaths per 100 million vehicle travel miles.*

Copyright Claimed 2017

That is, roughly 10^{-8} deaths/mile.[14] If we multiply that by 100,000 miles (likely less than most people travel in cars during their lifetimes), we obtain a lower limit of 10^{-3} for an individual's *lifetime risk of automobile fatality* and likely a factor of 10^{-2} for professional drivers (i.e., million-mile drivers). *Presented another way, if the USEPA regulated automobile transportation the way they regulate cancer risk, a person would not be allowed to travel more than 1000 miles by car in their lifetime!* With a 10^{-3} life-time risk of fatality, most of us will have personally known someone killed in a traffic accident during our lifetime.[15]

The situation is actually even more absurd. Transportation accidents take the lives of people independent of age. Indeed, many young people die and many these are not

---

[14] You can check these figures for the current year by looking up data from the US Department of Transportation.

[15] I have done analysis of loss of US bomber crews during WWII and found that up to about 3% (3×10^{-2}) losses *per mission* (i.e., 1 plane in 33 shot down on a mission) bomber- crew morale remained steady with a requirement of 20 to 50 missions. But, above this figure, ($20 \times 3 \times 10^{-2} = 0.60$) morale deteriorated and mission load had to be decreased.

Copyright Claimed 2017

voluntarily accepted risk[16]; they are unavoidable risk of everyday life. And the transportation data are based on actual "body counts" not hypothetical projections of models. Cancer death caused by regulated chemicals generally occur late in life (Albert *et al*, 1994). For example, the USEPA likes to use the original Taiwan arsenic study (Tseng, 1977; Tseng, 1989) because of the 40,000 people that give it statistical robustness. In these studies, most of the recorded skin cancer deaths were for people in their late stages of life. If you calculated lost life-years (e.g., 70 lost life-years = 1 fatality) rather than simple fatalities, the disparity in the cancer risk standard and transportation accident risk would be even more obvious.

Using *real* lifetime transportation risk (e.g., 10^{-3}) as a baseline, it seems unlikely that we will *never see any societal benefit* form regulations based on *hypothetical* risks that are regulated substantially more stringently (e.g., 10^{-5}) and mainly affect people beyond their working years (>60 years old). Parsing the risk into voluntary and involuntary categories is not realistic as automobile transportation is a universal fact of life. We have far more freedom to

---

[16] If a drunk driver crashes into you, you did not voluntarily accept the risk. Indeed, through your representatives, you specifically set standards for driving when intoxicated to reduce these risks.

Copyright Claimed 2017

discriminate in where we live, our careers, and our personal habits/tastes.

It seems to me that the proper place for setting a national risk target for cancer would be in the Congress by elected officials following a debate about the actual risk that we are expected to sustain and the benefits we might expect by trying to eliminate by regulating certain environmental exposures. As I will discuss in following sections, over-regulation of cancer distorts the economy, suppresses innovation and even increases overall risk.

The Adverse Impact of One-dimensional Risk Minimization

As argued above, the risk target for cancer from chemical exposure is roughly three orders of magnitude more stringent than other common risks. This distortion of our risk tolerance clearly has the effect of increasing overall risk. Using the CERCLA remedial process as an example, the ARARs are dominated by cancer-risk based drinking water MCLs and related risk targets. Thus, cancer risk drive the consideration for remediation of a contaminated site. Under CERCLA, no other type of risk is even considered. Thus, it is not unusual for an acceptable remedial design to require that thousands of cubic yards of (minimally contaminated) soil must be excavated, transported by road, treated and disposed and wells must be drilled and thousands of gallons of water pumped, treated and discharged to bring the risk at the site to *hypothetical* (i.e., currently nonexistent) residents of a parcel of land to the magic 10^{-6} lifetime risk targets. CERCLA does <u>not</u> require that (i) the risk to construction workers or (ii) people exposed to road accidents be considered. **CERCLA completely ignores these *real, current* sustained risks, which can easily exceed the *hypothetical, future* potential risk-reduction associated with some land occupancy scenario.** The situation is even more absurd from a rational risk management perspective when other *inappropriate* regulations are adopted as ARARs for the remedial design (see discussion above).

This effect carries over to impacts on the economy. For example, within the frame work of CERCLA, there is no formal consideration of the unit cost of risk reduction. Chemical contaminants tend to be distributed log-normally and the cost of remediation is driven by the amount of environmental media that must be manipulated rather than the amount of contaminant remediated. ***Thus, we can project that the cost of risk-reduction (and the risk associated with construction and transportation) increases exponentially as the risk target becomes more stringent.***

Page 42 of 61

Copyright Claimed 2017

It is easy to pick on CERCLA, but similar decisions are made under other environmental statutes. We mentioned earlier, the banning of DDT. Granted that the absolutely unrestricted use of DDT (circa 1960) threatened the extinction of various bird species. But, to completely ban a product (under FIFRA) that has saved so many lives from deadly disease (typhus, malaria, yellow fever) and could potentially save many more with the arrival of mosquito-borne diseases such as zika virus to North America seems absurd. More recently, the uses of chromated copper arsenate (CCA) wood preservative for dimensional-lumber used for decks and playground equipment (safely practiced for decades) was terminated because of the projected risk of cancer from arsenic. The combination of arsenic and copper in CCA provided a product that had 50 years of successful utility. It was replaced with products that had less desirable properties including leaching of higher levels of copper, which has higher aquatic toxicity. Also, if wooden structures fail because of accelerated decay (e.g., collapse of balconies or bulkheads) risk of injury is introduced.

Copyright Claimed 2017

Why is the Strict Cancer Risk Tolerance Accepted?

One might wonder why there has been no broad-based complaint against the risk standard applied to carcinogens. The answer is multifaceted and unexpected. First, cancer risk plays directly into obsessive compulsive OCD (chemophobic) inclinations shared to some degree by almost everyone in society (Gots, 1995). Indeed, in dogmatic repressive societies (e.g., Stalin's Russia or Hitler's Germany), the OCD behavior may be beneficial and "normal." Even the most objective observers are inclined to have reservations about risk causation that they cannot directly observe. Second, there is an unrelated "neopagan" element in society that sees pollution as a *religious* insult to the earth. Every time I see "Mother Nature" capitalized I cringe. In this ethical construct, pollution (of any sort and to any degree) is viewed as an unacceptable insult to the planet where "nature" takes on the status of a god. Absurdly restrictive standards (well beyond any practical impact) for environmental remediation or pollution prevention are consistent with a *feeling of guilt* for contaminating the gaian organism (Chopra & Lineweaver, 2016; Margulis & West, 1993).

On a more practical level, strict regulations regarding chemical exposure can be used as a political or economic

Copyright Claimed 2017

tool. Such regulations can be used to regulate consumption of natural resources; land use; all sorts of commercial activity; and even personal habits. These are, of course, the desires of socialist politicians.

Ironically, the general public has a misconception regarding the positions of profit-making industry and regulators. The popular assumption is that these two institutions are opposed to one another and the battle between the two during the promulgation of regulations is, thus, assumed by the public to represent some balanced compromise of risk and benefits. The *error* here is the notion that industry benefits from lax regulations. Indeed, *industry wants regulations!* Why? Well-established businesses like (environmental) regulations because those regulations create a barrier to entry into their market. *Industry is in the business of making a profit, not protecting the environment or defending rational risk-benefit analysis.* Industry ideally wants a regulatory regime that favors their product over competitors (e.g., aluminum utility poles over wooden poles treated with anti-microbial chemicals); but they will settle for a "level playing-field" for the *current* competitors with a barrier to entry by new competition. *Industry does not mind regulations (even strict regulations) provided the enforcement is predictable and uniform.* Whether the regulations make sense

Copyright Claimed 2017

from a risk-benefit perspective is irrelevant. Unpredictable, erratic and uneven enforcement is what industry loathes.

Indeed, industry may look to regulations to improve profitability. For example, I was the Director of Environmental and Regulatory Affairs for the American Wood Preservers Institute (AWPI) at the time the USEPA implemented a new arsenic risk assessment (2000-2002), which greatly restricted the use of chromated copper arsenate (CCA) in lumber used for decks and playground equipment. CCA works great as a wood preservative; in its 60 years in the market there had never been a serious complaint about its safety or effectiveness; it is easy to apply and easy to check quality; and it is very cheap. Indeed, well established standards for its application had been imposed by the American Wood Preservers Association (AWPA, a scientific body) and CCA was *no longer under patent*. These things made CCA-treated wood a very low profitability product for the industry. It was a *generic* product that anyone could produce and competition was brutal with hundreds of small wood treaters and three competing chemical companies supplying CCA. As the "big box" home-improvement stores evolved, these numerous small producers were competing for large contracts with national store chains and it all came down to the lowest bidder. The

Copyright Claimed 2017

"big box" stores used the wood as a lost leader (selling near cost) to get contractors to come in and buy expensive tools and hardware.

By 2000, the wood-treating industry was in paralysis and could do nothing about it. If you have ever been to a trade association meeting, you know that one of the first announcements made is that the participants are not to discuss pricing as that would violate laws against price fixing. And, of course, you could not fix prices without risking going to jail. Fortunately, the USEPA saved the industry by banning the use of CCA in these markets.[17] By banning CCA, EPA facilitates the introduction of non-generic (i.e., branded) products that *never before could compete on price or efficacy…and which had no safety record*, but had the commercial advantage of not-containing arsenic. In the end, the AWPI was actually disbanded by the industry in 2003 (in part, I believe, for AWPI's vigorous legal challenge of EPA in support of CCA).

---

[17] EPA's action was precipitated by formally applying the LNT cancer risk assessment based on the Taiwan studies to arsenic circa 1998. Because arsenic naturally occurs in ground water (e.g., Yellowstone National Park is a gigantic source of arsenic in natural water) the drinking water standards had been based on other criteria.

Copyright Claimed 2017

Summary

One could argue that, overall, very strict regulations spur innovation. And, that is probably true, but there is no guarantee that the innovative product *per se* will offer overall a better risk-benefit solution.

Strict application of a one-dimensional regulation against a single category of risk (i.e., life-time risk of cancer) distorts the preferred options and may actually increase overall risk with no discernable benefit. [For example, minimizing *calculated potential risk from hypothetical* chemical exposures while increasing *real current risk* from construction and traffic accidents.] Moreover, the innovation that is spurred by efforts to drive life-time cancer risk two or three order of magnitude below actual daily risks may introduce higher risk in some unexpected area and only create useful new knowledge as a serendipitous result of experimentation. Rather than bringing out the best in economic progress, over-regulation may encourage the worst.

Copyright Claimed 2017

Closing Comment

The environmental lobby, seems to be anticipating reversal of the cancer risk leverage in two different ways. First, they have built in "anti-backsliding" provisions into various laws. These provisions essentially say that once it has been demonstrated that industry can meet a standard, that standard will be maintained even if the reason for the standard evaporates. This may seem innocuous at the time the legislation is passed, but it may create a legislative roadblock to reasonable behavior at some later date.

Second, in the mid-1990s, the issue of "endocrine disrupters" with a non-linear dose-response was introduced. (Johnson, 1997; Tilson & Kavlock, 1997) The idea that we might observe effects at levels below which exposure could be detected opens a playground for claiming that any coincidental disorder may be blamed on some disrupter chemical. Several papers have been retracted (2009; 2015). Much of this research has centered on bisphenol A (BPA) (Marty *et al*, 2011). This was brought to the public's attention in 1996 (*Our Stolen Future, Are We Threatening Our Fertility, Intelligence and Survival? – A Scientific Detective Story* by Colborn et al.).[18] In principle, the

---

[18] Ironically, I had managed and led the development of the TSCA (section 4) test rules support document on BPA in 1984, where we had

Copyright Claimed 2017

environmental lobby (including socialists and earth religionists), may use endocrine disruption to cover a wider variety of chemicals and activities that can be reached with cancer. At least cancer is a objectively definable concept.

References

(1937) Mutation and the origin of cancer. *Cal West Med* **46**(1): 65-6

(1938) ELIXIR SULFANILAMIDE-MASSENGILL: Report of the United States Secretary of Agriculture. *Cal West Med* **48**(1): 68-70

(2009) Retraction. Transgenerational epigenetic imprinting of the male germline by endocrine disruptor exposure during gonadal sex determination. *Endocrinology* **150**(6): 2976

(2015) Retracted: Effect of melatonin administration and long day-length on endocrine cycles in the hedgehog Erinaceus europaeus. *Journal of pineal research* **59**(3): 402

Albert RE (1994) Carcinogen risk assessment in the U.S. Environmental Protection Agency. *Crit Rev Toxicol* **24**(1): 75-85

---

specifically called EPA's attention to the similar shape of BPA and estrogen and reported the few papers that purported estrogenic effects of BPA. At that time, EPA was not interested.

Copyright Claimed 2017

Albert RE, Benjamin SA, Shukla R (1994) Life span and cancer mortality in the beagle dog and humans. *Mech Ageing Dev* **74**(3): 149-59

Ames BN, Gold LS (1990a) Chemical carcinogenesis: too many rodent carcinogens. *Proc Natl Acad Sci U S A* **87**(19): 7772-6

Ames BN, Gold LS (1990b) Too many rodent carcinogens: mitogenesis increases mutagenesis. *Science* **249**(4972): 970-1

Auerbach C, Robson JM (1946) Chemical production of mutations. *Nature* **157**: 302

Berenblum I, Shubik P (1949) An experimental study of the initiating state of carcinogenesis, and a re-examination of the somatic cell mutation theory of cancer. *Br J Cancer* **3**(1): 109-18

Bitman J, Cecil HC, Harris SJ, Fries GF (1969) DDT induces a decrease in eggshell calcium. *Nature* **224**(5214): 44-6

Brookes P, Lawley PD (1964a) ALKYLATING AGENTS. *Br Med Bull* **20**: 91-5

Brookes P, Lawley PD (1964b) REACTION OF SOME MUTAGENIC AND CARCINOGENIC COMPOUNDS WITH NUCLEIC ACIDS. *J Cell Physiol* **64**: SUPPL 1:111-27

Brues AM (1958) Critique of the linear theory of carcinogenesis. *Science* **128**(3326): 693-9

Copyright Claimed 2017

Burdette WJ (1951) A method for determining mutation rate and tumor incidence simultaneously. *Cancer Res* **11**(7): 552-4

Burdette WJ (1953) The somatic mutation hypothesis of cancer genesis. *Science* **118**(3059): 196-7

Burdette WJ (1954) Somatic mutation and cancer. *Acta Unio Int Contra Cancrum* **10**(3): 97-104

Burdette WJ (1955) The significance of mutation in relation to the origin of tumors: a review. *Cancer Res* **15**(4): 201-26

Cai H, Kumar N, Bagheri HC, von Mering C, Robinson MD, Baudis M (2014) Chromothripsis-like patterns are recurring but heterogeneously distributed features in a survey of 22,347 cancer genome screens. *BMC Genomics* **15**: 82

Calabrese EJ (2013) Origin of the linearity no threshold (LNT) dose-response concept. *Arch Toxicol* **87**(9): 1621-33

Carr JG (1949) Chemical induction of mutation. *Biochem J* **44**(3): xvii

Chopra A, Lineweaver CH (2016) The Case for a Gaian Bottleneck: The Biology of Habitability. *Astrobiology* **16**(1): 7-22

Cohen SM, Arnold LL, Beck BD, Lewis AS, Eldan M (2013) Evaluation of the carcinogenicity of inorganic arsenic. *Crit Rev Toxicol* **43**(9): 711-52

Copyright Claimed 2017

Cuttler JM (2009) Commentary on Using LNT for Radiation Protection and Risk Assessment. *Dose Response* **8**(3): 378-83

D'Alessandro U, Buttiens H (2001) History and importance of antimalarial drug resistance. *Trop Med Int Health* **6**(11): 845-8

de Pagter MS, Kloosterman WP (2015) The Diverse Effects of Complex Chromosome Rearrangements and Chromothripsis in Cancer Development. *Recent Results Cancer Res* **200**: 165-93

Dewitt JB, Derby JV, Jr., Mangan GF, Jr. (1955) DDT vs. wildlife; relationships between quantities ingested, toxic effects and tissue storage. *Journal of the American Pharmaceutical Association American Pharmaceutical Association* **44**(1): 22-4

Dick DA (1978) The distribution of sodium, potassium and chloride in the nucleus and cytoplasm of Bufo bufo oocytes measured by electron microprobe analysis. *J Physiol* **284**: 37-53

Fernandez-Banet J, Lee NP, Chan KT, Gao H, Liu X, Sung WK, Tan W, Fan ST, Poon RT, Li S, Ching K, Rejto PA, Mao M, Kan Z (2014) Decoding complex patterns of genomic rearrangement in hepatocellular carcinoma. *Genomics*

Forment JV, Kaidi A, Jackson SP (2012) Chromothripsis and cancer: causes and consequences of chromosome shattering. *Nat Rev Cancer* **12**(10): 663-70

Copyright Claimed 2017

George JL, Mitchell RT (1947) The effects of feeding DDT-treated insects to nestling birds. *Journal of economic entomology* **40**(6): 782-9

Gots RE (1995) Multiple chemical sensitivities--public policy. *Journal of toxicology Clinical toxicology* **33**(2): 111-3

Haddow A (1974) Sir Ernest Laurence Kennaway FRS, 1881-1958: chemical causation of cancer then and today. *Perspect Biol Med* **17**(4): 543-88

Hadorn E, Niggli H (1946) Mutations in Drosophila after chemical treatment of gonads in vitro. *Nature* **157**: 162

Hayflick L, Moorhead PS (1961) The serial cultivation of human diploid cell strains. *Exp Cell Res* **25**: 585-621

Henkler F, Stolpmann K, Luch A (2012) Exposure to polycyclic aromatic hydrocarbons: bulky DNA adducts and cellular responses. *EXS* **101**: 107-31

Hoel DG, Kaplan NL, Anderson MW (1983) Implication of nonlinear kinetics on risk estimation in carcinogenesis. *Science* **219**(4588): 1032-7

Johnson GE, Doak SH, Griffiths SM, Quick EL, Skibinski DO, Zair ZM, Jenkins GJ (2009) Non-linear dose-response of DNA-reactive genotoxins: recommendations for data analysis. *Mutat Res* **678**(2): 95-100

Copyright Claimed 2017

Johnson J (1997) Endocrine disrupter research reviewed by EPA. *Environ Sci Technol* **31**(5): 221a

Klapacz J, Pottenger LH, Engelward BP, Heinen CD, Johnson GE, Clewell RA, Carmichael PL, Adeleye Y, Andersen ME (2016) Contributions of DNA repair and damage response pathways to the non-linear genotoxic responses of alkylating agents. *Mutation research Reviews in mutation research* **767**: 77-91

Kloosterman WP, Hoogstraat M, Paling O, Tavakoli-Yaraki M, Renkens I, Vermaat JS, van Roosmalen MJ, van Lieshout S, Nijman IJ, Roessingh W, van 't Slot R, van de Belt J, Guryev V, Koudijs M, Voest E, Cuppen E (2011) Chromothripsis is a common mechanism driving genomic rearrangements in primary and metastatic colorectal cancer. *Genome Biol* **12**(10): R103

Lewis DR, Southwick JW, Ouellet-Hellstrom R, Rench J, Calderon RL (1999) Drinking water arsenic in Utah: A cohort mortality study. *Environ Health Perspect* **107**(5): 359-65

Liu LY, Zheng J, Kong C, An J, Yu YX, Zhang XY, Elfarra AA (2016) Characterization of the Major Purine and Pyrimidine Adducts Formed after Incubations of 1-Chloro-3-buten-2-one with Single-/Double-Stranded DNA and Human Cells. *Chem Res Toxicol*

Lutz WK (1998) Dose-response relationships in chemical carcinogenesis: superposition of different mechanisms of action, resulting in linear-nonlinear curves, practical thresholds, J-shapes. *Mutat Res* **405**(2): 117-24

Copyright Claimed 2017

Magee PN, Schoental R (1964) CARCINOGENESIS BY NITROSO COMPOUNDS. *Br Med Bull* **20:** 102-6

Margulis L, West O (1993) Gaia and the colonization of Mars. *GSA today : a publication of the Geological Society of America* **3**(11): 277-80, 291

Marty MS, Carney EW, Rowlands JC (2011) Endocrine disruption: historical perspectives and its impact on the future of toxicology testing. *Toxicol Sci* **120 Suppl 1:** S93-108

Menzie CM (1972) Fate of pesticides in the environment. *Annual review of entomology* **17:** 199-222

Meyerson M, Pellman D (2011) Cancer genomes evolve by pulverizing single chromosomes. *Cell* **144**(1): 9-10

Moore FD, Sastry KS (1982) Intracellular potassium: 40K as a primordial gene irradiator. *Proc Natl Acad Sci U S A* **79**(11): 3556-9

Moore NW, Walker CH (1964) ORGANIC CHLORINE INSECTICIDE RESIDUES IN WILD BIRDS. *Nature* **201:** 1072-3

Morrison CD, Liu P, Woloszynska-Read A, Zhang J, Luo W, Qin M, Bshara W, Conroy JM, Sabatini L, Vedell P, Xiong D, Liu S, Wang J, Shen H, Li Y, Omilian AR, Hill A, Head K, Guru K, Kunnev D, Leach R, Eng KH, Darlak C, Hoeflich C, Veeranki S, Glenn S, You M, Pruitt SC, Johnson CS, Trump DL (2014) Whole-genome sequencing identifies genomic heterogeneity at a nucleotide and chromosomal level in bladder cancer. *Proc Natl Acad Sci U S A* **111**(6): E672-81

Copyright Claimed 2017

Muller HJ (1928a) The Measurement of gene mutation rate in Drosophila, its high variability, and its dependence upon temperature. *Genetics* **13**(4): 279-357

Muller HJ (1928b) The Production of Mutations by X-Rays. *Proc Natl Acad Sci U S A* **14**(9): 714-26

Nordling CO (1955) Evidence regarding the multiple mutation theory of the cancer-inducing mechanism. *Acta Genet Stat Med* **5**(2): 93-104

Odum WE, Woodwell GM, Wurster CF (1969) DDT Residues Absorbed from Organic Detritus by Fiddler Crabs. *Science* **164**(3879): 576-7

Oliver CP (1930) The effect of varying the duration of X-ray treatment upon the frequency of mutation. *Science* **71**(1828): 44-6

Olovnikov AM (1996) Telomeres, telomerase, and aging: origin of the theory. *Exp Gerontol* **31**(4): 443-8

Orgel LE (1965) The chemical basis of mutation. *Adv Enzymol Relat Areas Mol Biol* **27**: 289-346

Peakall DB (1969) Effect of DDT on calcium uptake and vitamin D metabolism in birds. *Nature* **224**(5225): 1219-20

Peakall DB (1972) Polychlorinated biphenyls: occurrence and biological effects. *Residue reviews* **44**: 1-21

Copyright Claimed 2017

Pollycove M, Feinendegen LE (1999) Molecular biology, epidemiology, and the demise of the linear no-threshold (LNT) hypothesis. *C R Acad Sci III* **322**(2-3): 197-204

Prendergast GC (2008) Immune escape as a fundamental trait of cancer: focus on IDO. *Oncogene* **27**(28): 3889-900

Preston RJ (2003) The LNT model is the best we can do--today. *J Radiol Prot* **23**(3): 263-8

Przybytkowski E, Lenkiewicz E, Barrett MT, Klein K, Nabavi S, Greenwood CM, Basik M (2014) Chromosome-breakage genomic instability and chromothripsis in breast cancer. *BMC Genomics* **15**(1): 579

Ratcliffe DA (1967) Decrease in eggshell weight in certain birds of prey. *Nature* **215**(5097): 208-10

Rau EP (2005) Combat science: the emergence of Operational Research in World War II. *Endeavour* **29**(4): 156-61

Risebrough RW, Rieche P, Peakall DB, Herman SG, Kirven MN (1968) Polychlorinated biphenyls in the global ecosystem. *Nature* **220**(5172): 1098-102

Rupert CS (1962) Photoenzymatic repair of ultraviolet damage in DNA. I. Kinetics of the reaction. *J Gen Physiol* **45**: 703-24

Copyright Claimed 2017

Spencer WP, Stern C (1948) Experiments to test the validity of the linear r-dose/mutation frequency relation in Drosophila at low dosage. *Genetics* **33**(1): 43-74

Stephens PJ, Greenman CD, Fu B, Yang F, Bignell GR, Mudie LJ, Pleasance ED, Lau KW, Beare D, Stebbings LA, McLaren S, Lin ML, McBride DJ, Varela I, Nik-Zainal S, Leroy C, Jia M, Menzies A, Butler AP, Teague JW, Quail MA, Burton J, Swerdlow H, Carter NP, Morsberger LA, Iacobuzio-Donahue C, Follows GA, Green AR, Flanagan AM, Stratton MR, Futreal PA, Campbell PJ (2011) Massive genomic rearrangement acquired in a single catastrophic event during cancer development. *Cell* **144**(1): 27-40

Swenberg JA, Bogdanffy MS, Ham A, Holt S, Kim A, Morinello EJ, Ranasinghe A, Scheller N, Upton PB (1999) Formation and repair of DNA adducts in vinyl chloride- and vinyl fluoride-induced carcinogenesis. *IARC scientific publications*(150): 29-43

Tang MH, Dahlgren M, Brueffer C, Tjitrowirjo T, Winter C, Chen Y, Olsson E, Wang K, Torngren T, Sjostrom M, Grabau D, Bendahl PO, Ryden L, Nimeus E, Saal LH, Borg A, Gruvberger-Saal SK (2015) Remarkable similarities of chromosomal rearrangements between primary human breast cancers and matched distant metastases as revealed by whole-genome sequencing. *Oncotarget*

Tarone RE (2015) RE: Is Bad Luck the Main Cause of Cancer? *J Natl Cancer Inst* **107**(10)

Tilson HA, Kavlock RJ (1997) The workshop on endocrine disrupter research needs: a report. *Neurotoxicology* **18**(2): 389-92

Copyright Claimed 2017

Tomasetti C, Vogelstein B (2015) Cancer etiology. Variation in cancer risk among tissues can be explained by the number of stem cell divisions. *Science* **347**(6217): 78-81

Tseng WP (1977) Effects and dose--response relationships of skin cancer and blackfoot disease with arsenic. *Environ Health Perspect* **19**: 109-19

Tseng WP (1989) Blackfoot disease in Taiwan: a 30-year follow-up study. *Angiology* **40**(6): 547-58

Waddell WJ (2004) Dose-response curves in chemical carcinogenesis. *Nonlinearity Biol Toxicol Med* **2**(1): 11-20

Watson JD, Crick FH (1953a) Genetical implications of the structure of deoxyribonucleic acid. *Nature* **171**(4361): 964-7

Watson JD, Crick FH (1953b) Molecular structure of nucleic acids; a structure for deoxyribose nucleic acid. *Nature* **171**(4356): 737-8

Wax PM (1995) Elixirs, diluents, and the passage of the 1938 Federal Food, Drug and Cosmetic Act. *Annals of internal medicine* **122**(6): 456-61

Weinberg CR, Zaykin D (2015a) Is bad luck the main cause of cancer? *J Natl Cancer Inst* **107**(7)

Weinberg CR, Zaykin D (2015b) Response. *J Natl Cancer Inst* **107**(10)

Copyright Claimed 2017

Wilcox JM, Rempel DL, Gross ML (2008) Method of measuring oligonucleotide-metal affinities: interactions of the thrombin binding aptamer with K+ and Sr2+. *Anal Chem* **80**(7): 2365-71

Woodwell GM, Wurster CF, Jr., Isaacson PA (1967) DDT residues in an east coast estuary: a case of biological concentration of a persistent insecticide. *Science* **156**(3776): 821-4

Wyatt AW, Collins CC (2013) In Brief: Chromothripsis and cancer. *J Pathol* **231**(1): 1-3

Yasui M, Kanemaru Y, Kamoshita N, Suzuki T, Arakawa T, Honma M (2014) Tracing the fates of site-specifically introduced DNA adducts in the human genome. *DNA Repair (Amst)* **15**: 11-20

Yue L, Zhang Y, Chen J, Zhao Z, Liu Q, Wu R, Guo L, He J, Zhao J, Xie J, Peng S (2015) Distribution of DNA adducts and corresponding tissue damage of Sprague-Dawley rats with percutaneous exposure to sulfur mustard. *Chem Res Toxicol* **28**(3): 532-40

www.ingramcontent.com/pod-product-compliance
Lightning Source LLC
Chambersburg PA
CBHW020330290526
45785CB00007B/2988